Pockets
of
Heaven

Written by

PAULINE COLLIER

The Choir Press

Copyright © 2023 Pauline Collier

All rights reserved. No part of this publication may be reproduced or transmitted in any form or by any means, electronic or mechanical including photocopying, recording or any information storage or retrieval system, without prior permission in writing from the publishers.

The right of Pauline Collier to be identified as the author of this work has been asserted by her in accordance with the Copyright, Designs and Patents Act 1988

First published in the United Kingdom in 2023 by
The Choir Press

ISBN 978-1-78963-359-7

Dedicated to

Dawn Louise
Sharon
David
Bernadette
Garry
Louise
And
Friends

I have made *Pockets of Heaven* into a small book, which you can carry around with you at all times. Read this book when you have challenges going on in your life, or when you feel unloved, in need of upliftment or inspiration.

The words in *Pockets of Heaven* have been given to me from my guide, James. I hope this book will help in your time of need.

Our Father who art in heaven,
Hallowed be thy name.
Thy kingdom come
Thy will be done on earth, as it is in heaven.
Give us this day our daily bread.
And forgive us our trespasses,
as we forgive those who trespass against us,
and lead us not into temptation,
but deliver us from evil.
For thine is the kingdom
the power and the glory
forever and ever.
Armen.

My Introduction to Spirit

I am the middle child of three. I was brought up on a council estate with my mum, dad, my granddad and two brothers. My dad was a train driver, which he loved. My mum stayed at home until we were old enough for her to go out to work, as a part-time cleaner at St Luke's Hospital in Rugby.

In between having two sons I met an old school friend I hadn't seen since we were teenagers. She told me how she lost her son. I listened to her story; it changed my life and brought me back to our Creator.

When I left work, I thought what am I going to do with myself? I was used to getting up early, meeting people I had known for years, until one morning I woke up feeling out of sorts. I lit a candle and put on some relaxing music and closed my eyes; it wasn't long before I saw and heard someone talking in my mind, giving me my first ever story.

God and the talking tree. I opened my eyes and for a few seconds I saw my family in spirit waving to me.

Since then, I have had stories after stories gifted to me from spirit. Now I have been asked to write this book. It will be up to you if you believe me or not. I write what I am given, not what I think.

These are pockets of heaven from some of my experiences.

My visions from the angels and spirit which I have been allowed to share with you.

When I think of these pockets of heaven I am shown, it like opening a door to another world. When I talk about love, I cannot justify the love I feel, it was so powerful.

The first time this happened to me I found myself in a forest. The animals that I write about were waiting for me, waving to me wanting me to join them. Fairies and elves watching me; at times like this I want to stay. The feeling of freedom to laugh, no cares, no worries, just enjoyment to be you. Everything is alive, the trees, the flowers, then I come back to this heavy world.

✧ ✧ ✧

When we go to heaven, we create a life like we have here on earth. We can also move into other people's pockets of heaven. These are people we have loved and have met on earth. These people are in your soul family.

I have seen angels walking up steps together towards large see-through buildings. I have seen angels surrounded by bright lights coming down from heaven sending out rays of love upon this world. Being told that they walk among us, giving us our Creator's love. I have seen children playing having fun, laughing together amongst the long grass; one came over to me and smiled. The freedom, no crying, no fighting or arguing. I thought how wonderful that children who have passed are enjoying themselves, meeting other children playing just like they do here on earth.

※ ※ ※

After I moved into a bungalow not long ago, feeling extra tired I went and sat on my bed. As I sat a loud voice spoke to me; it was strong but kind asking me to lie down and not to move. As I lay, I felt I was in a wind tunnel, it was so strong. I lay there for what seemed an age thinking it was never going to stop. But when it did, I lay there thinking, what has just happened to me? Then I was shown a picture of heaven on my wall; I sat up and said, 'How beautiful.' I stood up and moved towards it when I bumped into my dressing table. I asked a friend of mine what it all meant.

She told me I was visited by an archangel; I was being cleansed of my negativity ready to start my new chapter in my life.

My Mind is Calm

I have monks shuffling along a large hall saying. 'This way please.'

We walk to a large door that opens into another room, where a lady is holding a tray of tea waiting for me. 'Come sit. Have a cup of tea.' I sit down and take a sip. My mind relaxes and I start to dream.

I am in a large hallway floating along, people are waving saying, 'Hello, long time no see.' They recognize me. Along I go; this hall is endless.
I hear the sound of a gong and everyone disappears. A man appears. 'Do I know you?' I ask.

'Yes, but don't think, just let it all unfold; close your eyes.'

The man offers me a drink. 'Drink this; it will free your mind,' he said.

I take a sip and sit just being; the man is talking but my mind is elsewhere.

What a journey this life has been and is.

A box is put in front of me with a pink bow on top. 'Open it,' I'm told.

As I touch the ribbon it has a life of its own. I watch the ribbon unfold the box opens and out pours all my deeds and misdeeds before me.

I sip the tea; my mind is calm. I don't have any feelings towards any.

I hear a song in my mind, it won't be long now.

I'm on a boat floating; the sea is calm, I'm not alone.

'We have read your mind, we give you calm waters, love and joy to the end.'

The sky opens up to the bluest blue, my feet on green grass, when a voice says,

'Would you like a cup of tea?'

I'm back.

'Yes please,' I reply.

Walking Our Journey

When we are going through difficult times, most of us ask the spirit for help. I class this as our journey of life. When you are born and take your first breath, your journey has begun. The path is there for us to walk from the beginning to the end.

You will find different roads; some are bumpy others smooth. You will come across forks and have to make a choice which way to go. I tend to look at this as a maze, the twists and all the dead ends while trying to find the end. These twists are choices we make; some lead to nowhere, and we say, 'I shouldn't have done that,' or, 'why did I do that?'

Whatever happens on these twists or choices are lessons, not mistakes, as we call them. There are no mistakes, only lessons. We carry on until we find our way back onto our path. The sun comes out, the waters are calm, yes you have found peace and happiness life is good. Until temptations lure you off your path to enlightenment and it starts all over again, but you will always find your way home in the end.

I wonder what you will say to your family in spirit when you return home. I might say, 'Wow, what a journey that was. I will try harder next time.' Yes next time.

Smile

Have you ever felt the love of God inside you?

You are out walking along a path when you come across a man or woman who has just fallen down. What do you do? Walk on by. No! At that moment in time your heart stirs, you have a need to help this person.

You stop and talk to them; you help them stand up if they can. Other people come rushing over. 'Can we help,' they ask?

This man or women thanks you for your care. It makes you feel warm inside.

'I have done a good deed today,' you say to yourself and carry on walking.

This is how we should feel every day. We should have that feeling every moment of the day. We all have a part to play, say, 'Hello,' with a smile when you are out walking. It doesn't matter if they don't reply or smile back. Say it every time you meet them. Eventually they will smile and say hello to you.

What a part you have played, to have opened someone's heart even if it is just for that moment. Think of the chain reaction you have started.

Trust

I try to meditate, but find it hard to settle, when I hear a voice talking to me.

I am but a child sitting next to a waterfall. The voice is asking, 'What are you waiting for, are you going to jump?' I move closer to the edge. The waterfall is deep, I cannot see the bottom, only water falling.

'Well, are you going to jump?' I am asked again.

In my head I hear myself counting, one, two, three, then I stop at the edge, the fear has come. 'What stopped you? Why are you fearful?' I am asked.

'Trust, put your trust in me; the angels are waiting to catch you.'

I give myself a shake and say, 'This time.' I move back; then I start to run, and as I take that leap of faith, I can feel the love and joy enfold me. Yes, the angels were waiting to catch me, don't let the fear take over your life; put your trust in our Creator and your life will be stronger, more loving and more joyful.

As I lay, the angels come and stand around me singing. Archangel Michael opens his wings and lays them over me, putting me into a bubble of protection. An eagle stands next to me watching me grow from a child to a woman. The angels stop singing and clap their hands which sends shockwaves around this world, taking away the old, bringing in the new ways of living.

Mother Earth

Closing my eyes, I find myself sitting on a cliff top; I am but a child crying.

An eagle comes flying towards me asking, 'Why are you crying, little one?'

'I am crying for the world,' I reply.

'Climb on my back, I have something to show you,' said the eagle.

Flying in the air I see the world and all that mankind has done. The world is sick; at that moment I have a need inside me to help heal the world. The eagle lands and stands over me while I sleep. I hear music and the warmth of the earth lulls me to sleep.

Mother Earth is smoothing me while singing her songs. I can feel her pain; the music is so loving. When I wake, I say my prayers to our Creator in the heavens, asking for guidance and how to heal the earth to take away the pain from Mother Earth.

As I sit the eagle stands by my side listening to my prayers. 'Will they listen?' he asks.

I implore the children to send love to Mother Earth and the world; to have respect and to do their best to teach the elders and to show them the new ways; to stop the greed and the wanting, to live in love and harmony with each other.

I close my eyes and look ahead at what the world could be; the grass is green, nature is alive, the sky is blue. I can hear the laughter of mankind. I open my eyes and look at the eagle, 'Yes,' I said, 'I have been shown what this world could be if we all stand together and stop those who don't believe.'

Coats of Negativity

I light a candle and say a prayer; I put my music on; sit down and close my eyes. I find myself drifting to a far-off land, when I come across an Native American pulling faces at me. He is laughing at me.

I open my eyes to see my grandfather in spirit before me. He looks full of love for me; I feel a little taken a back in fear of being ridiculed. I have not meditated for a long while; I feel ashamed.

My body feels heavy for I am wearing layers of coats. Grandfather says, 'Let's go home.'

'Will they greet me?' I ask. 'It has been a long time.'

'You will not be allowed into the camp until you shed your coats of negativity,' he says.

We start to walk; I listen to him talking to me. I start to feel lighter. I shed a coat, then another and another. Grandfather is still talking to me. I feel younger. I want to dance; my coats are still falling away. I see the camp up ahead; some women come and give us water to drink. I say, 'Thank you.' We carry on walking. Still my coats are falling away; my heart feels like it wants to sing. I run to the doorway until I can't run any more. Grandfather comes and picks me up; I am a newborn baby. I am naked. Now I am allowed into the camp.

Ask the Angels for Help

When I watched my mother ascend to heaven. I saw an angel put her hand on my mum's shoulder. The angel did not look like what I have been taught – all angels have wings, but there were no wings. When you need to be strong, they give you the male strength and when you have a need to be loved or to be nurtured, they give out the female side of them.

The angel was wearing a shroud just like my mother. This was my mum's guardian angel, who was with her all her life.

I have seen an angel with wings, very large wings. His feathers were perfect like a bird's wings but bigger. He was dressed all in white with dark hair. I felt blessed.

You might ask, 'Who is she? What does she know?' Nothing, I only know what I am told by spirit, and what I experience through visons.

When I am ill, or when I am going through rough periods in my life, I talk to my guardian angel asking for help, making wishes as we do, or just talking.

Angels are all around us. We all have our own guardian angel or angels, who are with us when we are born. We are very privileged.

When you feel down or low, talk to your guardian angel. All you have to do is ask. Your guardian angel is with you wherever you go, talking to you inspiring you, sending you love.

Put your trust in them.

When we are born, we come with a purpose, but as we don't remember we have to work it out for ourselves. When I am writing I am living with my forest and field animals with the elementals. You might laugh, and so would I have years ago. I have come so far, and have found why I am here on this journey we call life. This is my destiny.

Put Your Trust in Our Creator

This world of ours is changing, and sometimes we feel not always for the better. Go with the flow, be good, be kind to each other and believe in the Creator. Please do not let the dark seduce you. There is only one Creator, believe and put your trust in him. When you wake up in the morning and open your eyes; say thank you for giving me this day.

It's a new day, live it, enjoy it!

The Meeting Place

Closing my eyes, my mind starts to wonder. I am at the meeting place where my guide Simon is waiting to take me to the monastery in the sky.

'Have you brought water and a bar of chocolate as I asked?' he says.

'Yes,' I reply, as I bring them out of my rucksack.

I notice the air is heavy. I put on my pointed sun hat and start to walk.

'It's a long way up,' I say.

'You can do this,' he say. 'One step at a time.'

I can feel the sweat beads on my forehead as we continued walking upwards.

At this point the path is clear quite easy to walk, but the heat is nearly too much to bear.

'Can we stop?' I ask.

Simon turns and takes a look at me. 'We shall stop just for a few moments, take a drink and one square of chocolate. Let it melt on your tongue,' he says.

Sitting on a boulder, I take a look around me. I can see the treetops and the

lagoons so blue. 'What a sight,' I think.

It wasn't long before Simon says, 'It's time to move on.'

I put my water and chocolate away and as I put my rucksack onto my back, I take another look around me. Up we go. I don't look at my watch on purpose as time doesn't matter.

I look down at the path. Little stones are lying in our way. 'Don't look at them,' says Simon. 'This road may get rougher before we get there.' The little stones start to get bigger, just as he said.

'Simon,' I ask, 'have you done this journey before?'

'Not this one, but others are quite hard.

Harder than this one,' he puts in, which makes me feel better in myself.

Up we go. The air is getting lighter and my body feels full of energy instead of heavy. 'Shall we stop for a moment?' says Simon. 'Have another drink and one piece of chocolate. Don't forget let it melt on your tongue.'

I do as I was told. The last of the treetops are showing themselves to me, as the clouds are taking their place.

'How are you feeling?' asks Simon.

'Good,' I answer. 'My body is getting used to the climb. I feel lighter and stronger.'

'Good,' he replies, with a smile.

Up we go. I notice the big stones are disappearing and being replaced by the smaller ones again. 'Oh yes,' I said to myself the pathway is easier now. I look upwards, but still cannot see the monastery. 'How much further,' I ask Simon.

'Not far now,' he replies. 'Have another drink and a square of chocolate and don't forget.'

I step in, saying with a laugh, 'Let it melt on your tongue.'

I can only see the clouds now, white and fluffy all around us. 'Thank goodness for this pathway,' I say to myself.

Up we go drinking the water and eating one square of chocolate at a time, not talking much. My body feels lighter, but tied. I look up to see a glimmer of the beginnings of a building. Simon turns towards me.

'Can you see? We are nearly there.'

My heart beats faster, I want to run and shout we are here, we have made it. But the air is a lot thinner now I'm having a job to breath. I take the last of my water and the last square of chocolate letting it melt on my tongue. I feel it going down my throat. It feels strange. I have never had that before. I would put food in my mouth and down it went. But this is different.

'Come on,' shouts Simon. 'Can you see the door?'

Yes, two large doors stand in front of me shinning bright, with two monks standing there in red and orange cloths waiting to open them.

'Come,' they call.

I walk through the large doors to see rows of

monks sitting cross legged chanting. The air were heavy, but light at the same time. I can feel my body healing as I walk past them. I look for Simon but he is nowhere to be seen. I carry on walking. My back is straight, my legs are strong, still the monks carry on chanting om.

I reach the other end of the room where two more monks are standing next to another set of two doors.

'Are you ready?' says one, in a very clear voice.

'Yes,' I reply.

The two monks open the door and as they open a brilliant blue light starts to shine onto me. I can see the blue sky and the green grass.

'Go, go,' the monk says to me. 'It's your turn.'

I walk through, into this place. The sky is a brilliant blue and the grass a greener colour than I have ever seen before.

I stand looking around when I notice one of my feet is going into the ground. A voice speaks, 'Don't let that worry you, you have been on a long journey, a journey of your ups and downs. Your foot is into the earth while you decide what you want to do.'

'But why has my foot gone into the ground?' I ask.

'Why, you still have one foot on earth and one in heaven.'

I stand listening to what the voice is saying to me. 'So, it is my choice,' I answer, when the voice stops talking. I look at a film show in front of me showing how my family and friends will be without me.

'I have made my decision,' I say. 'I will go back to see my time out.'

I am out of the monastery and back at my meeting place with Simon.

'You did well,' he says, 'You have made the right choice.'

Then he is gone and now I am back, but what a journey it was.

Ask for Help for They Will Hear You

A man on horseback comes riding to me.

'Be careful Pauline, the Bear is on the rampage; he has got out of his cage.'

'What should I do? Hide.'

'No, he will find you, stand up, be tall and strong, you can do this.'

I stand still feeling sick, I can see the Bear running towards me.

I pray to God for help and guidance.

The Bear stops in front of me, standing on two feet beating his chest while giving out a loud roar.

I stand still, looking up to him.

I hear a voice asking me, 'What is wrong here?'

'He is frightened,' I ask.

'Nobody likes me,' he says.

'Well, if you go around roaring and standing over people, what do you expect?'

I say. 'Be good, be kind, be understanding to others' needs and above all don't roar. Do what I do, say a prayer, ask for help, ask God or the one you believe in and your family in spirit to help guide you.'

The Bear sits thinking. 'I will go know and do as you say.

You are stronger than you know,' says the Bear to me as he turns to go.

'Believe in yourself,' he calls out, and disappears.

So whatever life throws at you, face your fears; you can do it, you know. You are stronger than you think.

Feeling Different

We are all different, we all believe in different things. You see your friends and how they act, but this isn't you. You look at life differently. Everyone has things going on in their life, but what is going on with them is different to you. Their view on life; what they think or say, being good or bad to them is different to you. Stay true to yourself; don't compare yourself with others. You are on a different path. Don't let them tempt you and take you off your path, listen to your gut, your inner feelings.

Choices

The pain in my body is almost too much to bear. I sit and close my eyes. I hear music so calming, so soothing

I am floating, I am dying. I feel no pain, I feel free from everything that has been. I see my life before me, some of the pain I have caused and the loves I have lost.

My family, my friends, but how free I feel.

Time

What is time? No regrets or wish-I-had, or what-ifs, they just float away leaving peace and the feeling of freedom

My body has stopped hurting, all my pains have left me, what peace I have never known.

When I see angels coming to greet me; they take me to a flower garden while I wait my turn.

The colours of the flowers I have never seen before are so bright.

An angel comes and takes my hand, we go to a room. What love, what peace I feel.

'Where am I?' I ask.

'It's your turn know,' replied the angel.

I hear a voice say, 'We are love you are love, it's your choice to stay or go, you are in between. Close your eyes now. It's your choice.'

I close my eyes for a moment then I open my eyes, I can feel the pain in my body and the heaviest of life on my shoulders.

For I am back sitting down, I have made my choice.

Ascending

When my mum died, I felt despair. This woman who brought me into this world, who loved and cared for me, sharing all my problems, has gone and left me. My emotions were all messed up; I felt as though I was the only one going through this journey. Going to work, coming home and curling up on the settee not able to function.

Until one morning a month after my mum had died, my alarm sounded. I switched it off and closed my eyes. Then I heard a voice talking to me, 'God and the angels are coming.' I held onto my duvet, then it came again, 'God and his angels are coming.' I gripped my duvet even tighter when suddenly I was looking at a film. A crowd of people appeared of all ages wearing a shroud, looking up. I lay there looking at them all to see if I recognized anyone; then I saw my mum. She was standing still looking up; she looked younger and healthy. I tried to look up to see what they were looking at, but I couldn't see. I remember thinking, 'Look at me, Mum, I'm here,' but she kept looking up.

Then the angels appeared and stood next to each person with a hand on their shoulder. I was laying there saying out loud in my mind, 'I want an angel to put their hand on my shoulder.' Then they were gone.

I felt alone, I wanted to go with her so much. Then a man stepped forward holding a long scroll in one hand and a large pen in the other hand, and said, 'No Pauline, it is not your time, you still have a lot to do.' What, go to work? Do the house work? Exist? But now I know what he meant, what he was talking about. Years later I am writing children's stories and now this little book. How my life has changed.

Believe

When you pass to spirit, you will be overwhelmed with love, you cannot put this feeling into words. You will see your family who have passed – not just your immediate family, but also your friends who are in spirit.

If you pass with an illness, your soul may go to what we call here a hospital, to heal you; your soul will feel heavy as you have come from a heavy world. Or you may go straight to the gardens like the poem I wrote called Choices, where the angels will show you where you belong.

There is no reason to be frightened or worried. Whichever level you go to you will feel the love and be loved. The angels will show you a remote viewing of your journey here on earth; where you did well and where you could have done better. For those who didn't complete their journey, they will be given the opportunity to come back and try again.

I hear people saying, 'I don't want to come back,' as their soul will want to experience other challenges. Or they may go to other planets. It is a big universe out there.

Horse

As I sit listening to my Native American drumming music, my body goes still. I am not myself; I have changed.

I look down to see my legs so long and strong. I find myself galloping through the long grass on the plains.

Oh, the freedom; with the wind in my face, my hair is flying into the air.

My heart is pounding. I am alive!

The eagles circling high above, screeching to me before they carry on.

I stop at a stream and stand drinking water. It tastes so sweet as it runs down my throat.

I start to run and jump in circles while I start to dance and click my heels. Oh, the freedom I am feeling!

Looking up to the sun, it is time for me to go; I take another drink before I gallop back through the long grass, until that moment comes, I can see the encampment up ahead. How proud I feel; my heart is thumping.

As I enter the encampment, I start to trot, passing by the children playing, the old men sitting with their blankets around their shoulders.

They look up as I walk past them and smile.

Yes! What a life I live, I want this moment to go on forever.

Believe In Me

My dad was one of those people who did not believe. 'When you die, it's all black,' he used to say. When he was dying, he would call out to me and my brothers, 'Who are all these people? Get them out of here.' When he went into hospital he would shout, 'Get these children out of here,' but he still would not believe.

One morning when my dad was in a nursing home, my brother and I walked into his room. He was talking about things that had happened to him in his life. I suddenly realised, he was putting his life in order and we were there to help him, to put his mind at rest, not to judge. I knew he was not going anywhere until he had finished his book of life.

One morning he called for his mum. I knew it wouldn't be long before he joined them. I felt honoured that he had allowed us all to be part of his passing.

Freedom

The web is being weaved, one piece at a time. Round and round goes the spider checking all is well.

The spider carries on regardless. Nothing else matters at this moment in time.

If I catch my prey what a web this is going to be.

Is this our lives? People weave their web ready to catch us, knowing there is no escape.

Stand up, be strong, have courage. Bring all your strength to the fore.

We can beat them. Ask the universe, the angels and those in spirit who love us for help.

I ask for you to be true to yourself; so be brave, be strong, with love and faith you will be free.

As I have been writing this book with my guide, James, it has opened up my world. It has made me question what has happened in my own life; the choices I have made. The good times, the not so good. Yes, I have a lot of not so good and still do.

As I walk this path to enlightenment, I am finding it even harder. I am starting to see and feel the temptations that are out in front of me more so.

As we are still learning, all I can say to you who are reading this book; when choices come your way don't jump in, stop! Take your time, the spirit is here to help you find your pathway.

Don't forget you have to ask! They cannot help unless you ask them, because you have been given free will.

O thou, the breath, the light of all,
Let this light create a heart-shrine
Within and your council rule till oneness guides me,
Your one desire then acts with mine, as in all light so in all forms,
Grant what I need each day, in bread and insight,
Loose the cords of mistakes binding me,
as I release the strands I hold of other faults.
Do not let surface things delude me, but keep me from unripe acts.
To you belongs the ruling mind, the life that can act and do,
The song that beautifies all, from age to age it renews, in faith I will to be true.